I. M. Coloring Presents:

An Adult Coloring Book with Mandalas, Flowers, and other Patterns

I0468140

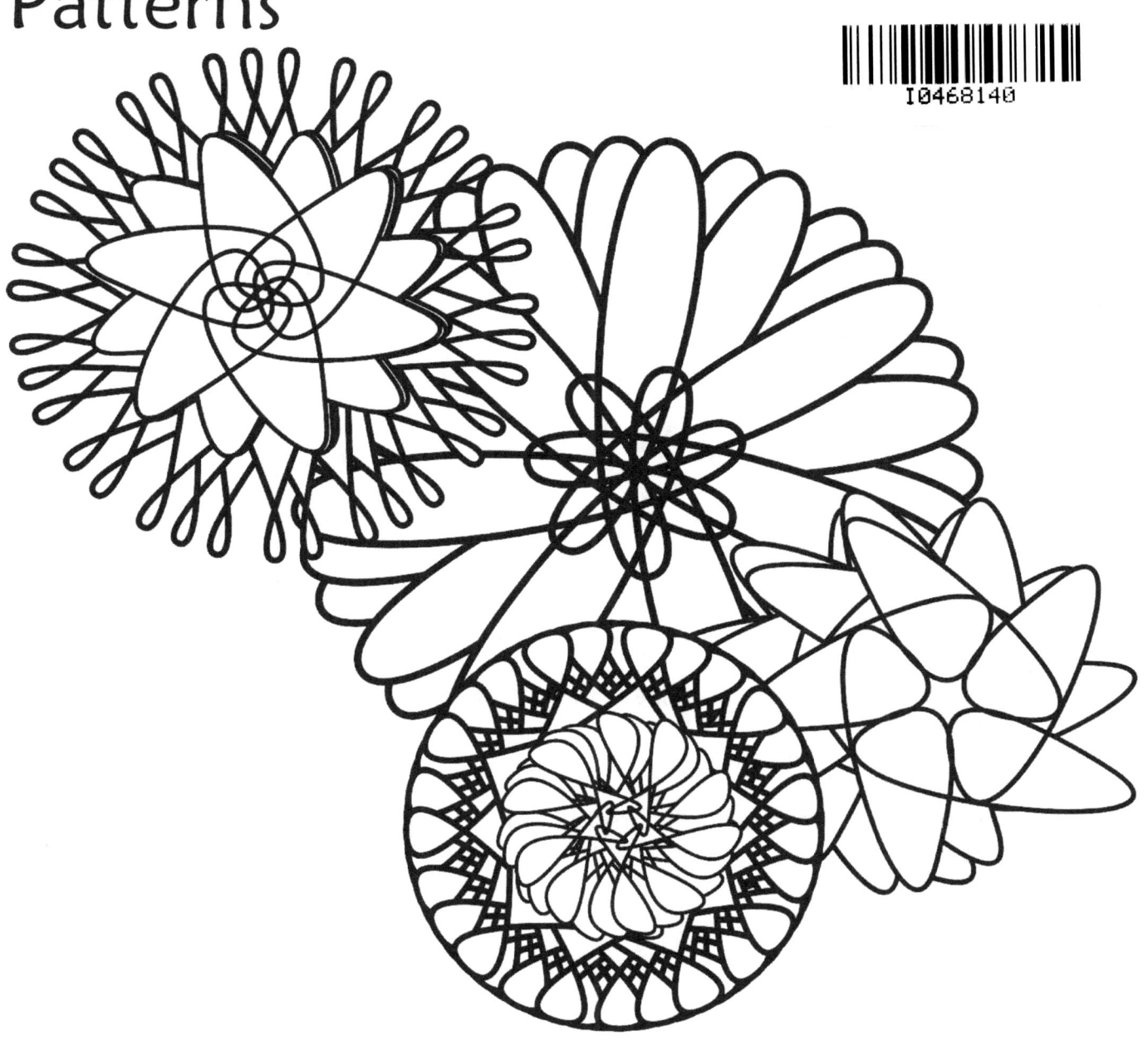

I. M. Coloring Presents:
An Adult Coloring Book with Mandalas, Flowers, and other Patterns
By I. M. Coloring
Copyright 2016 Don D. Cummings

ISBN-13: 978-1523674961

ISBN-10: 1523674962

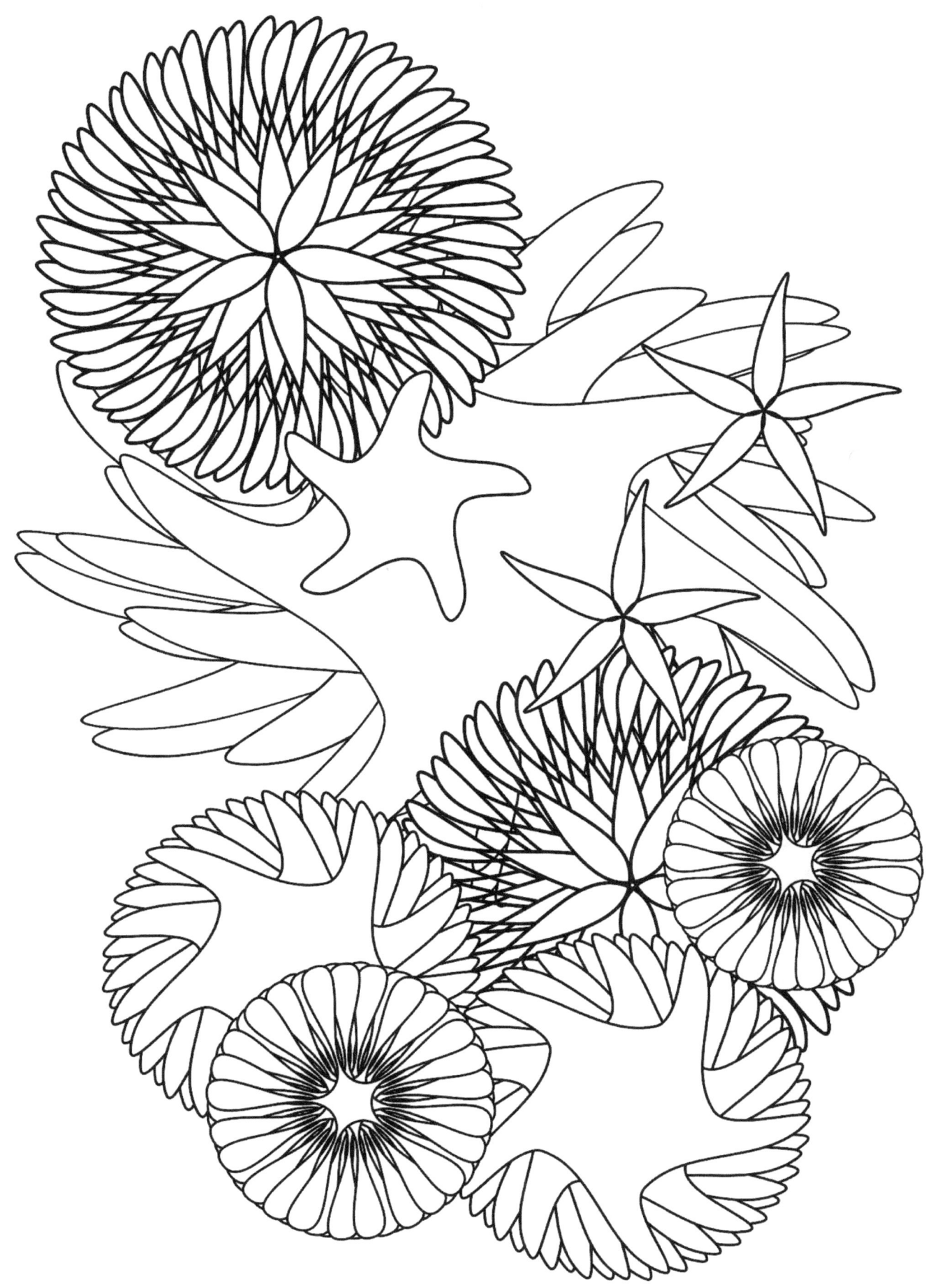

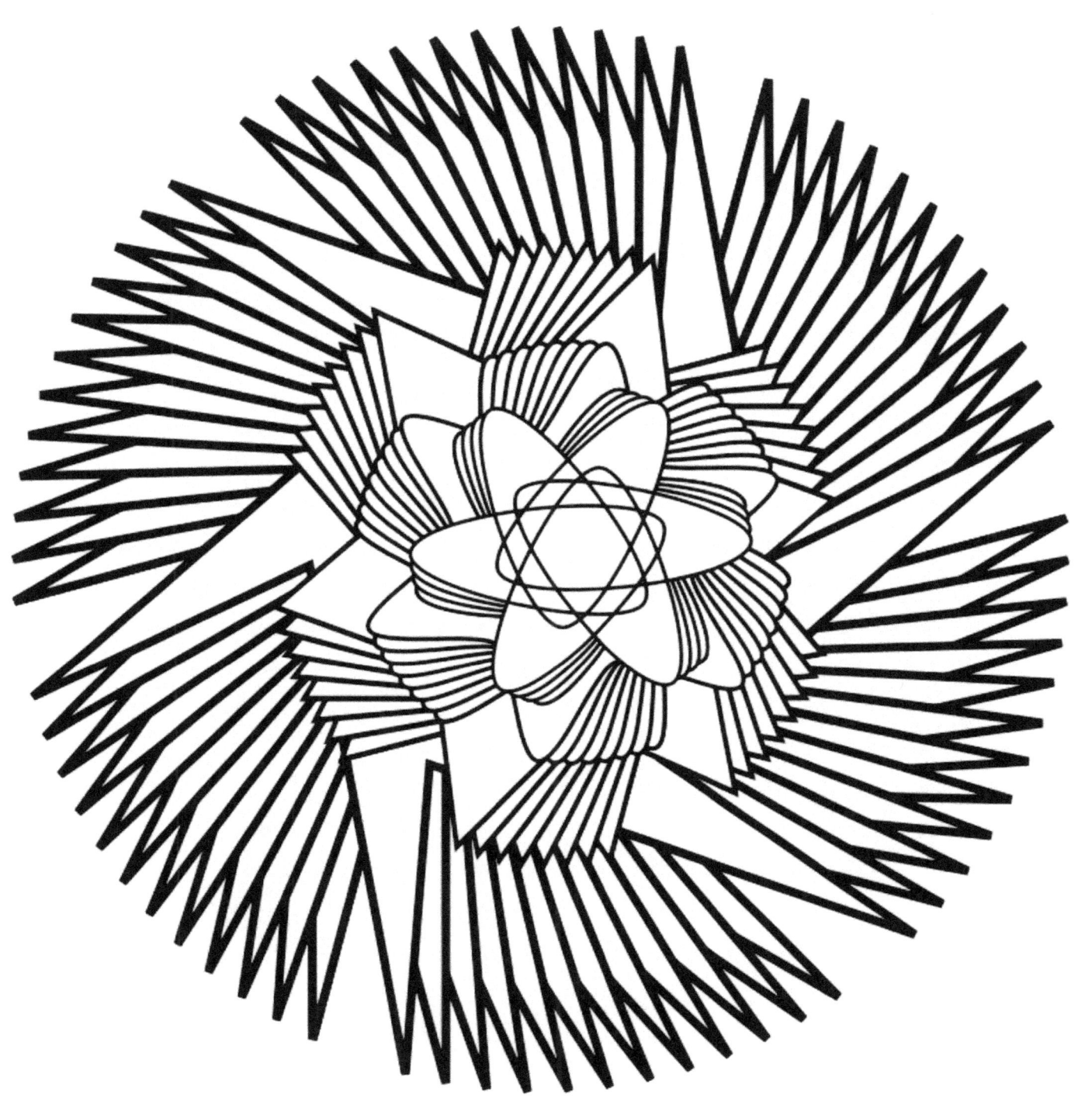

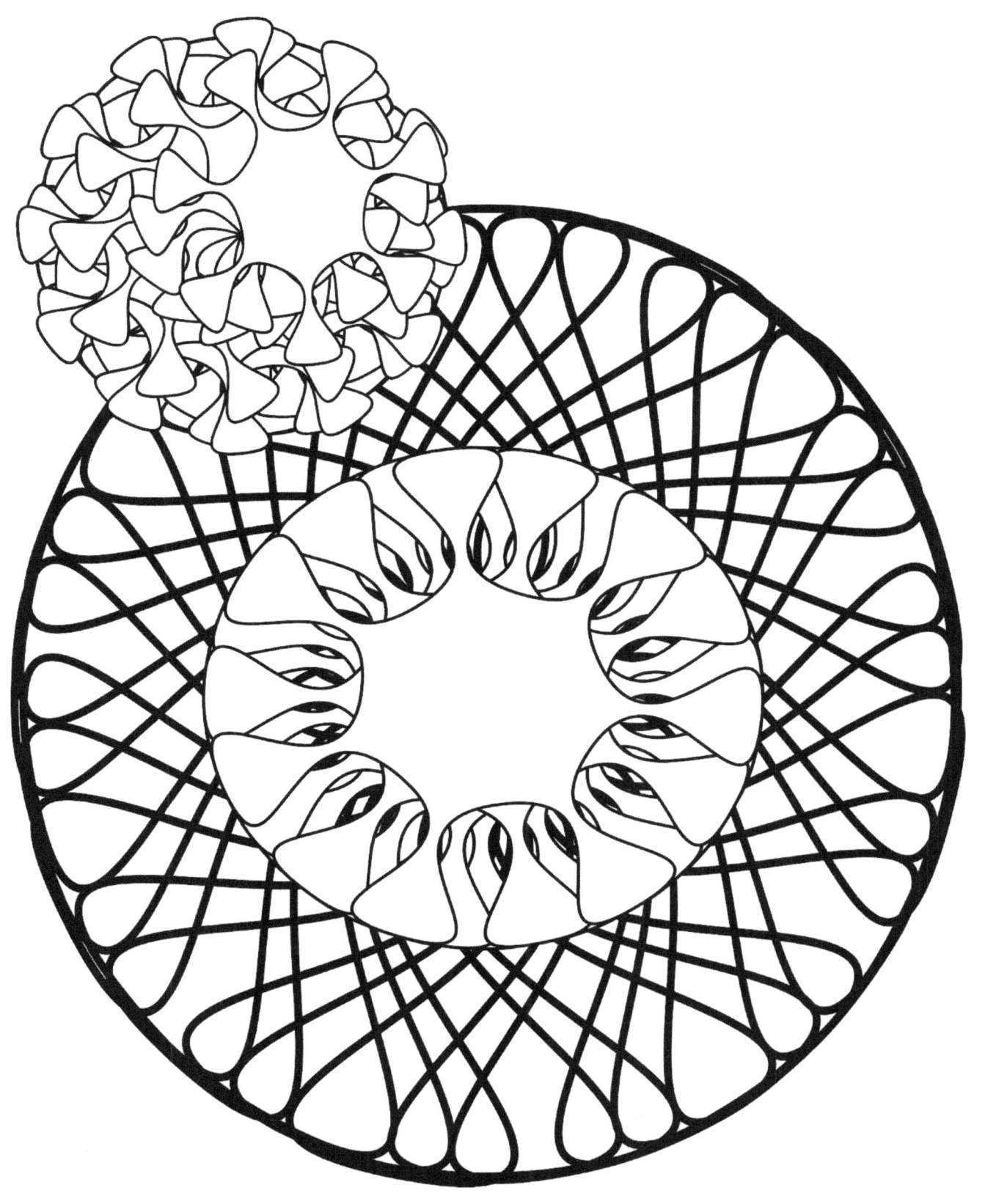

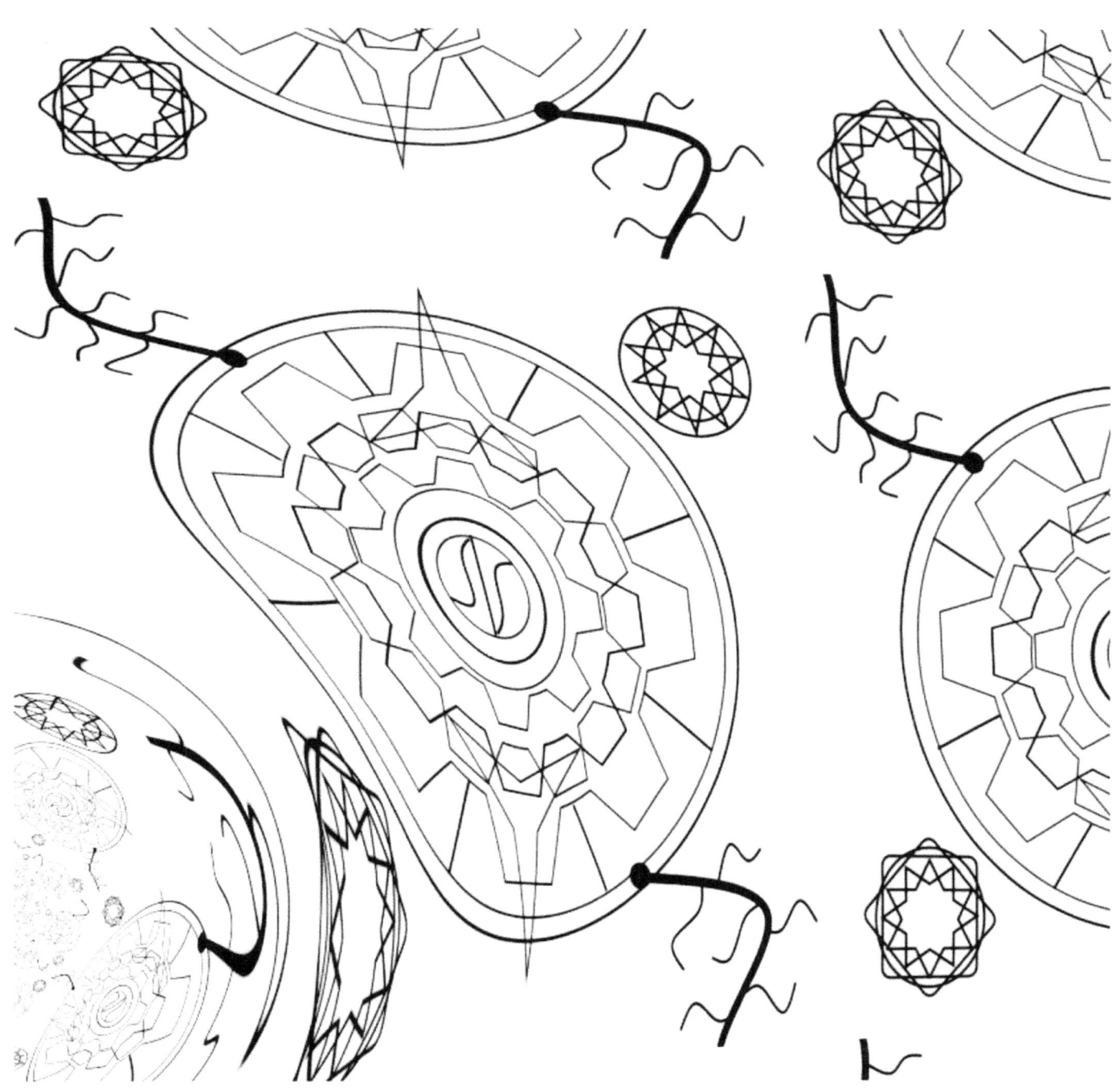

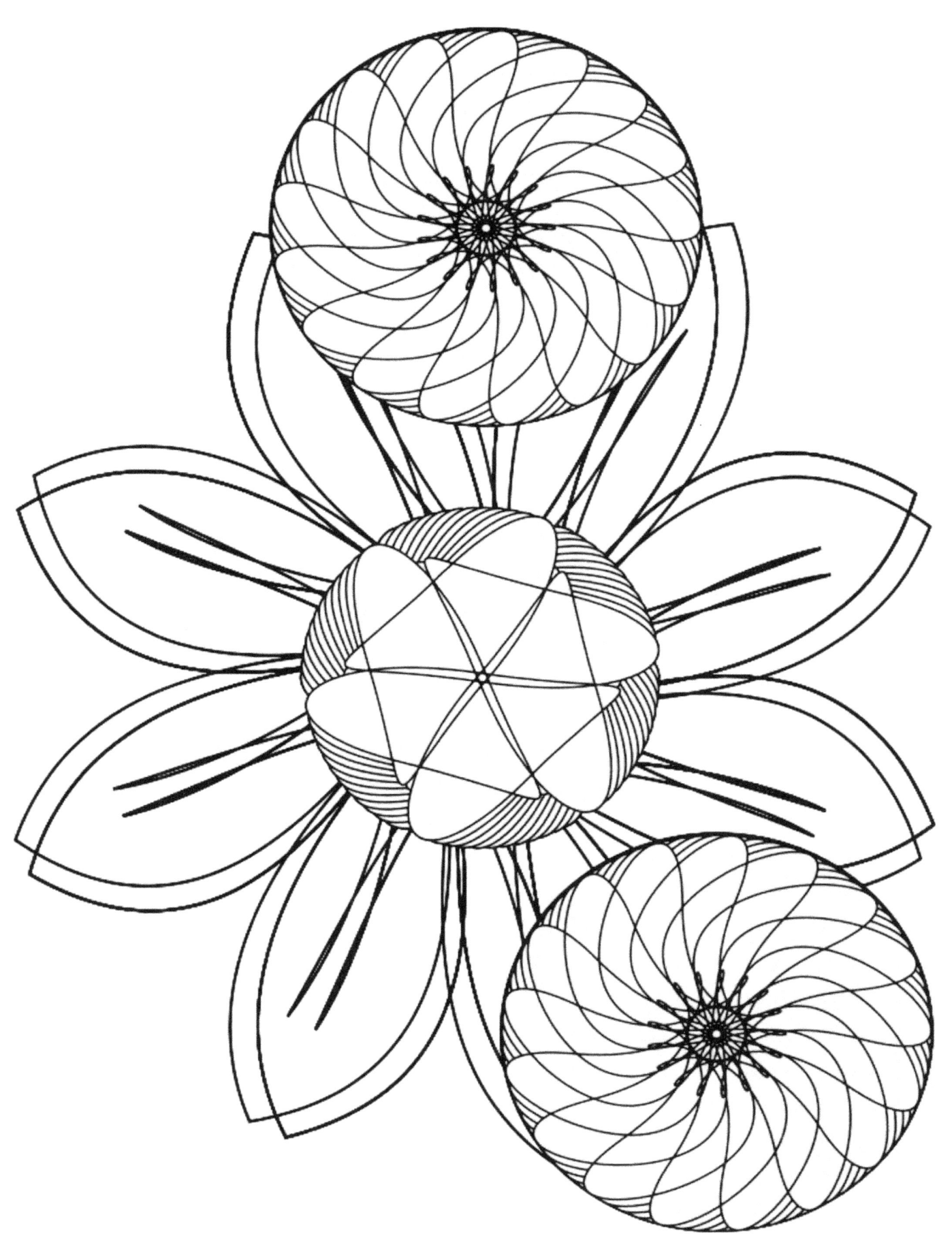

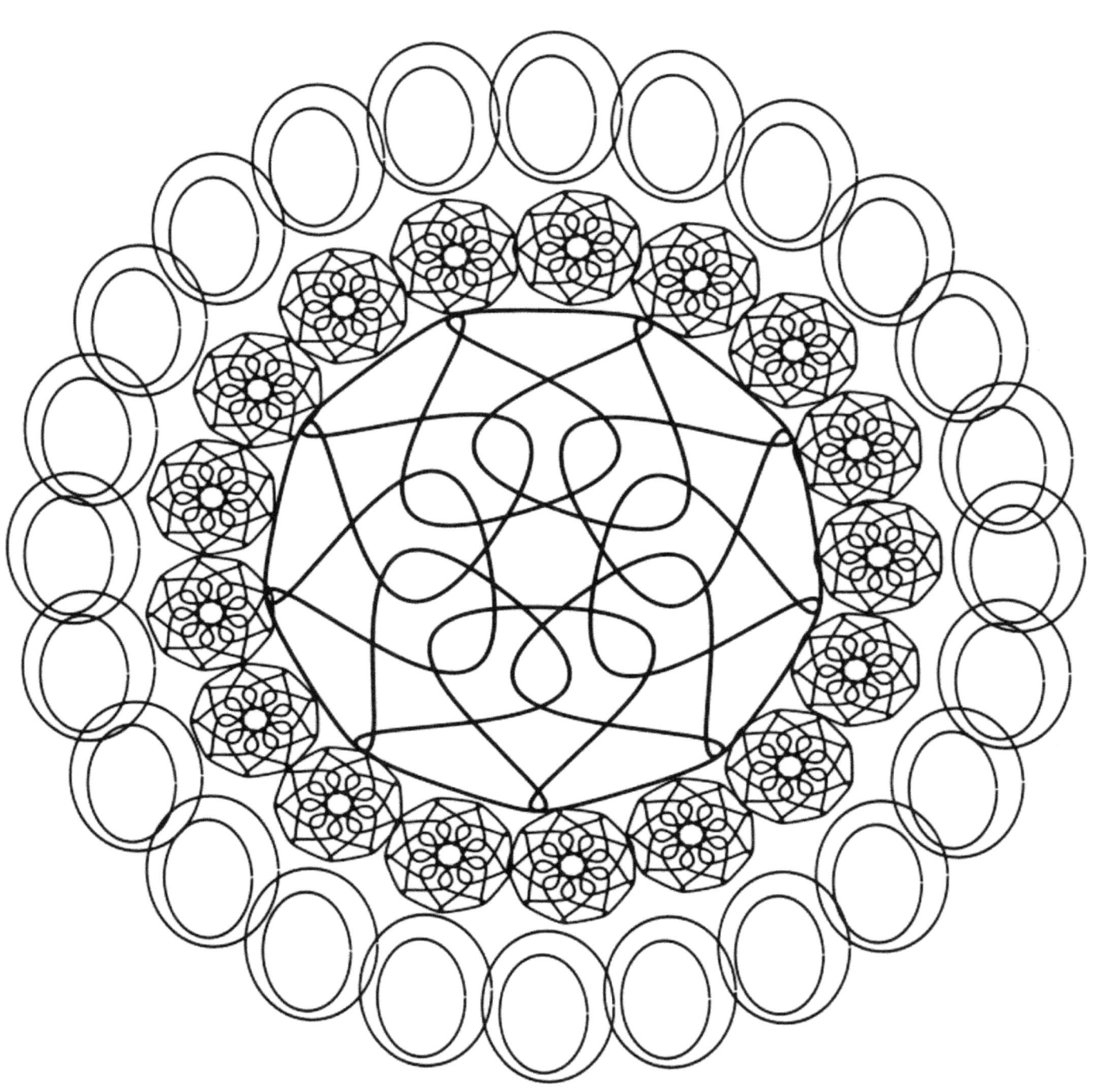

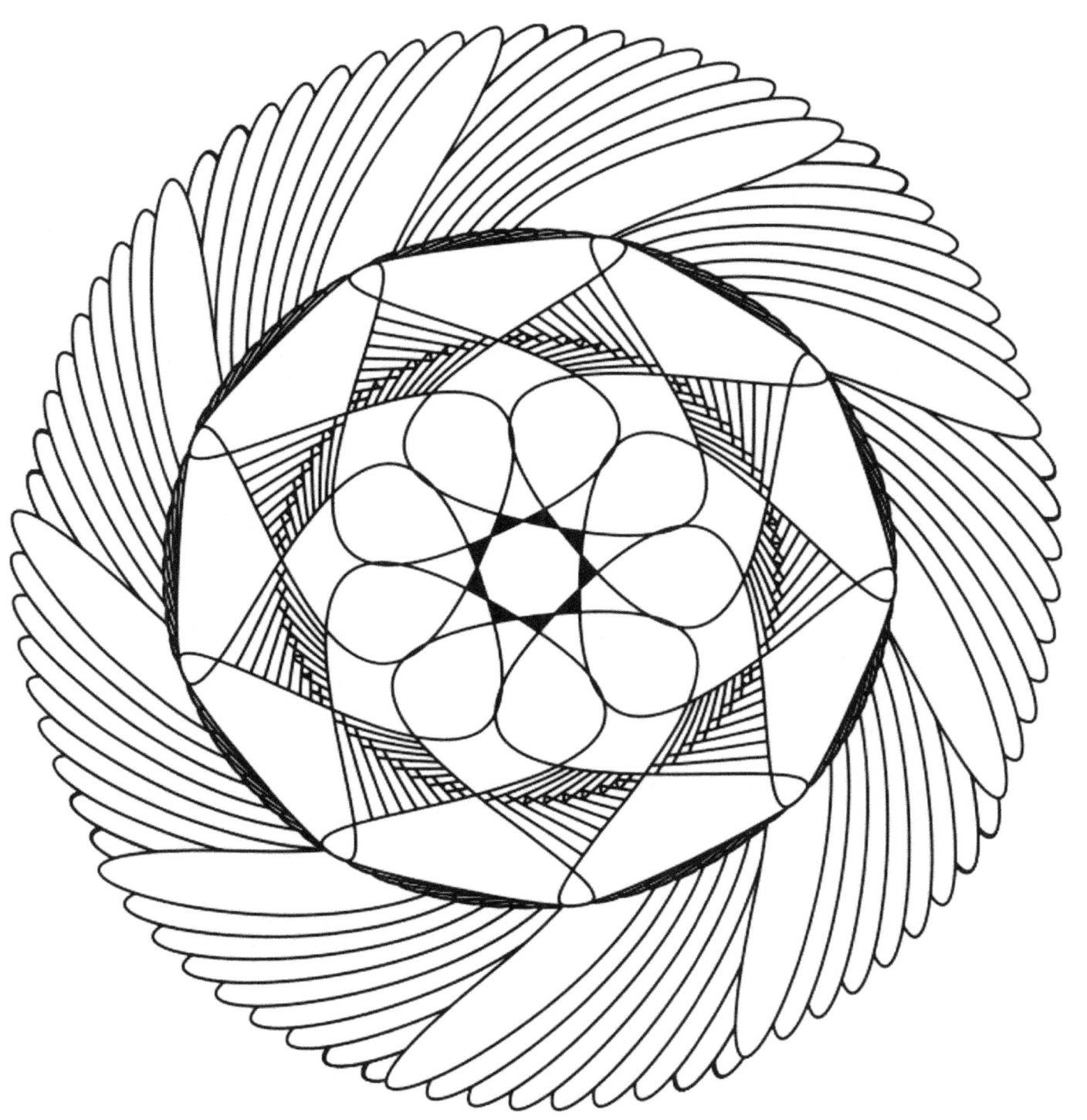

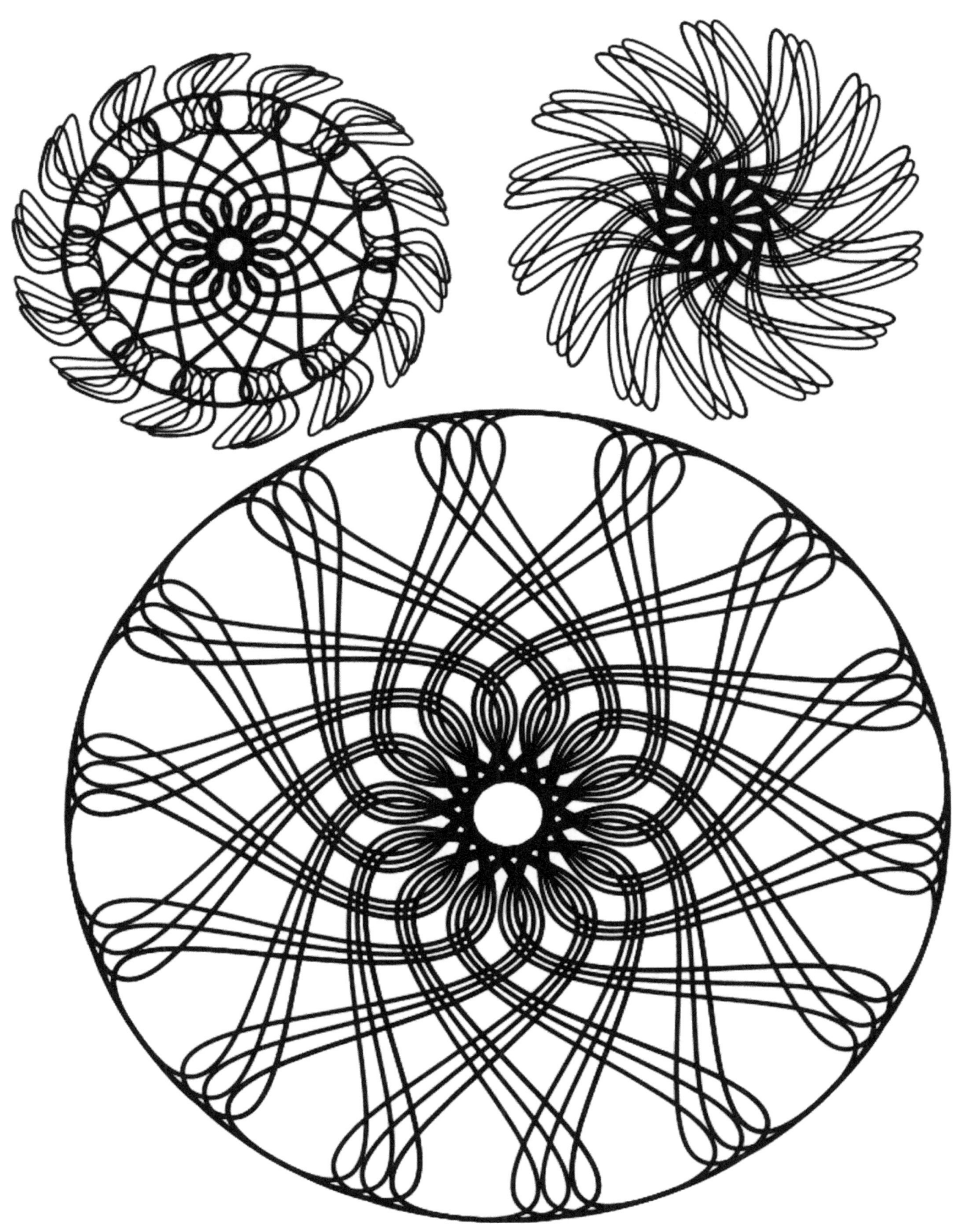

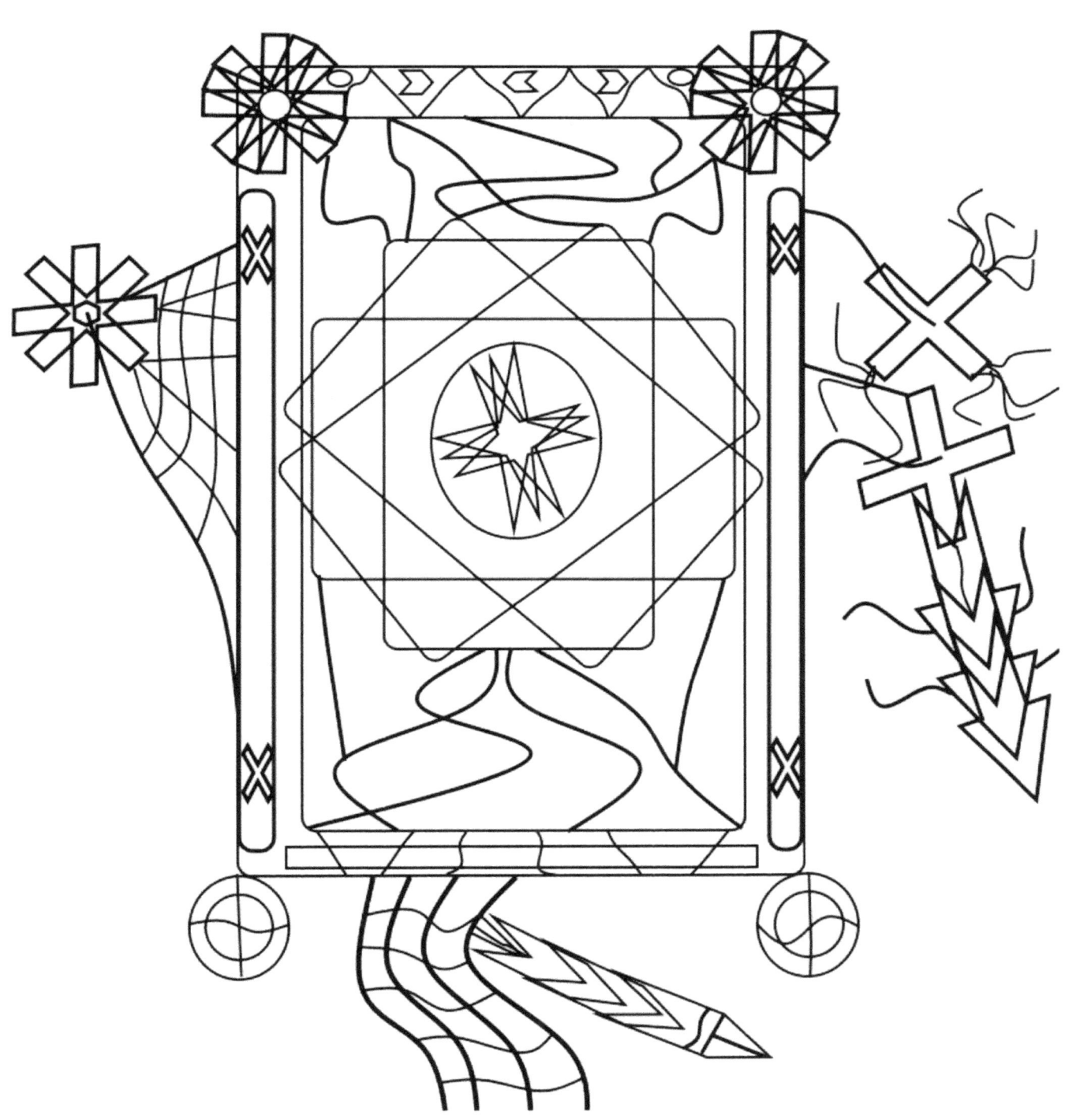

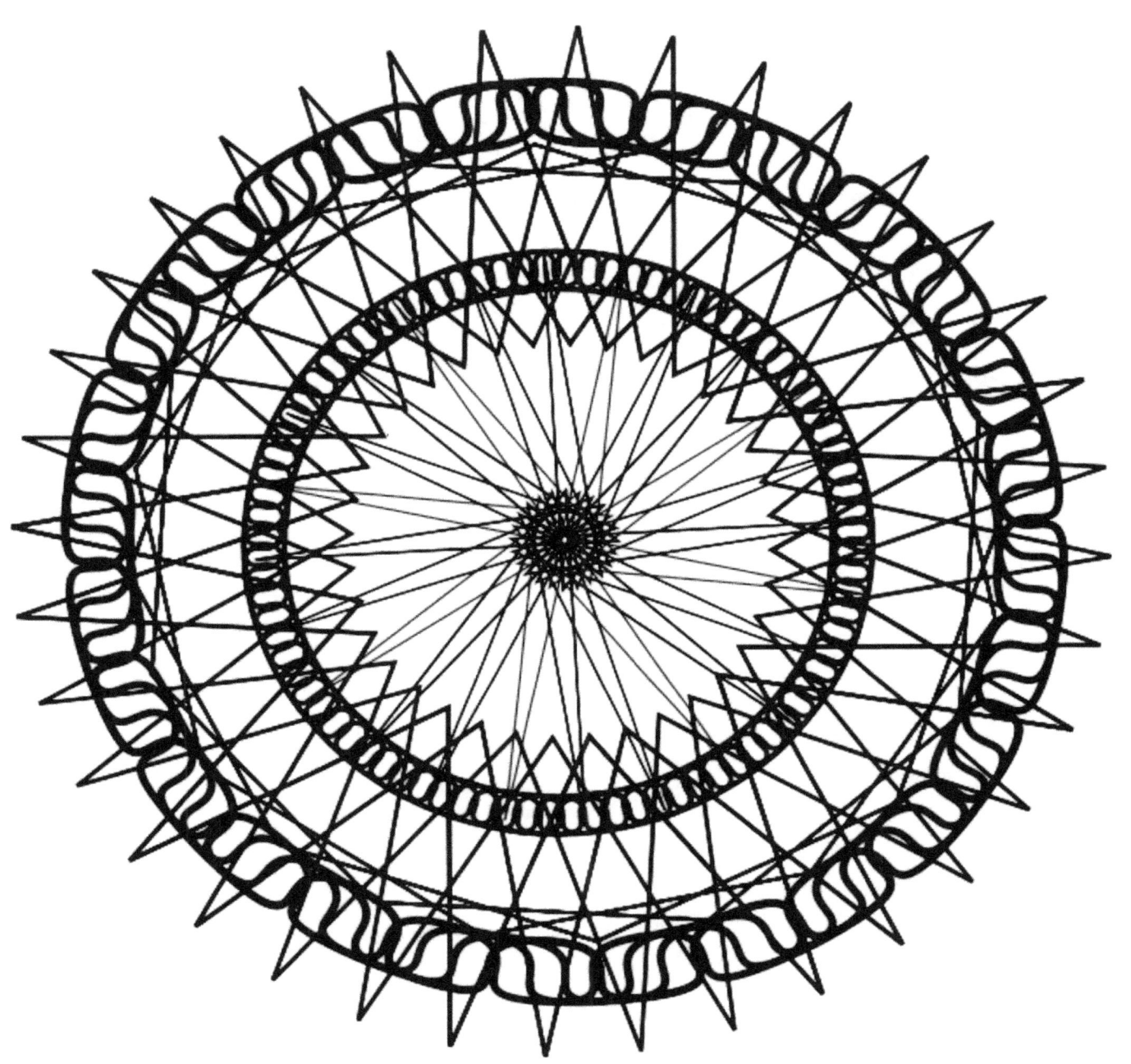

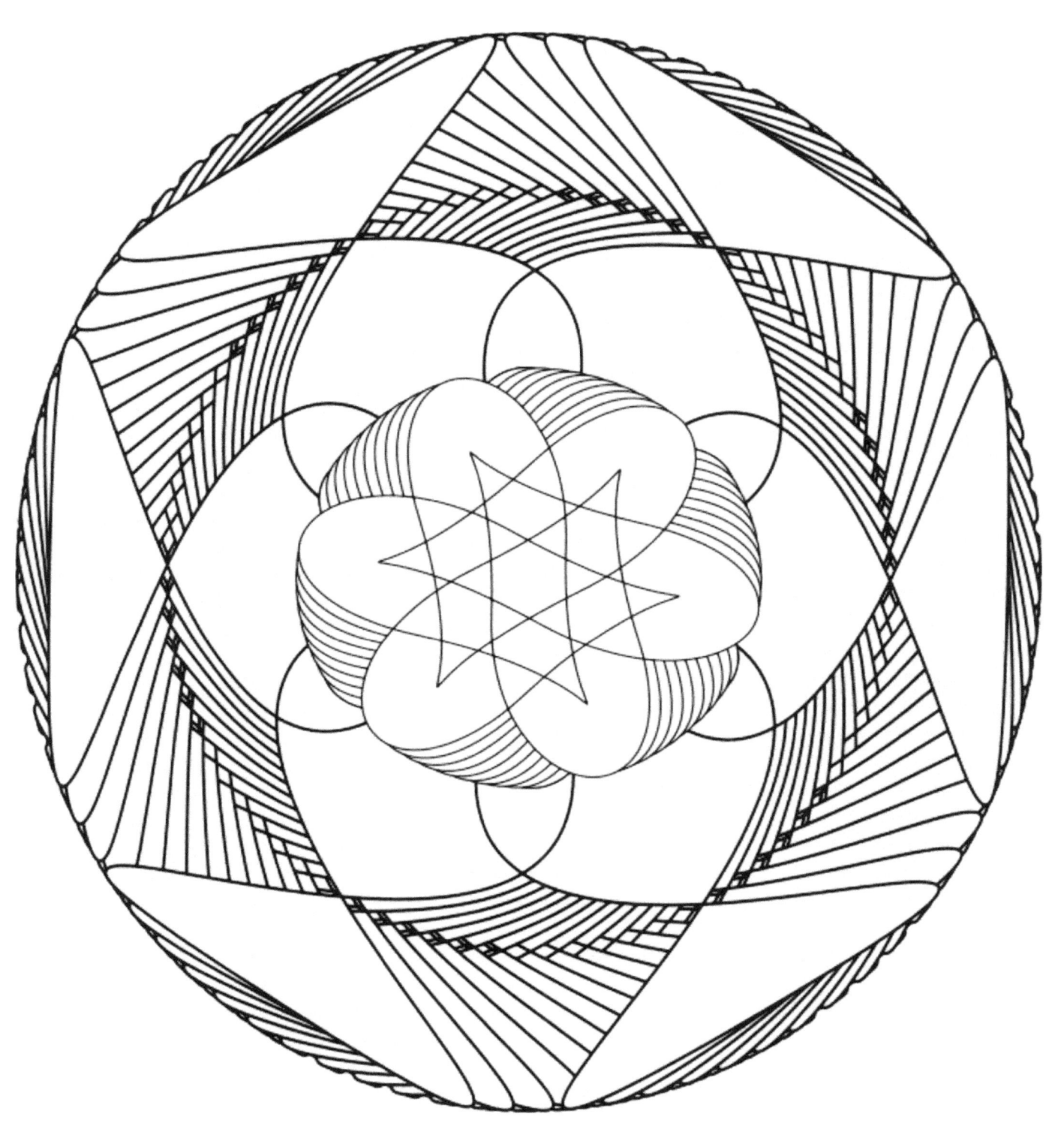

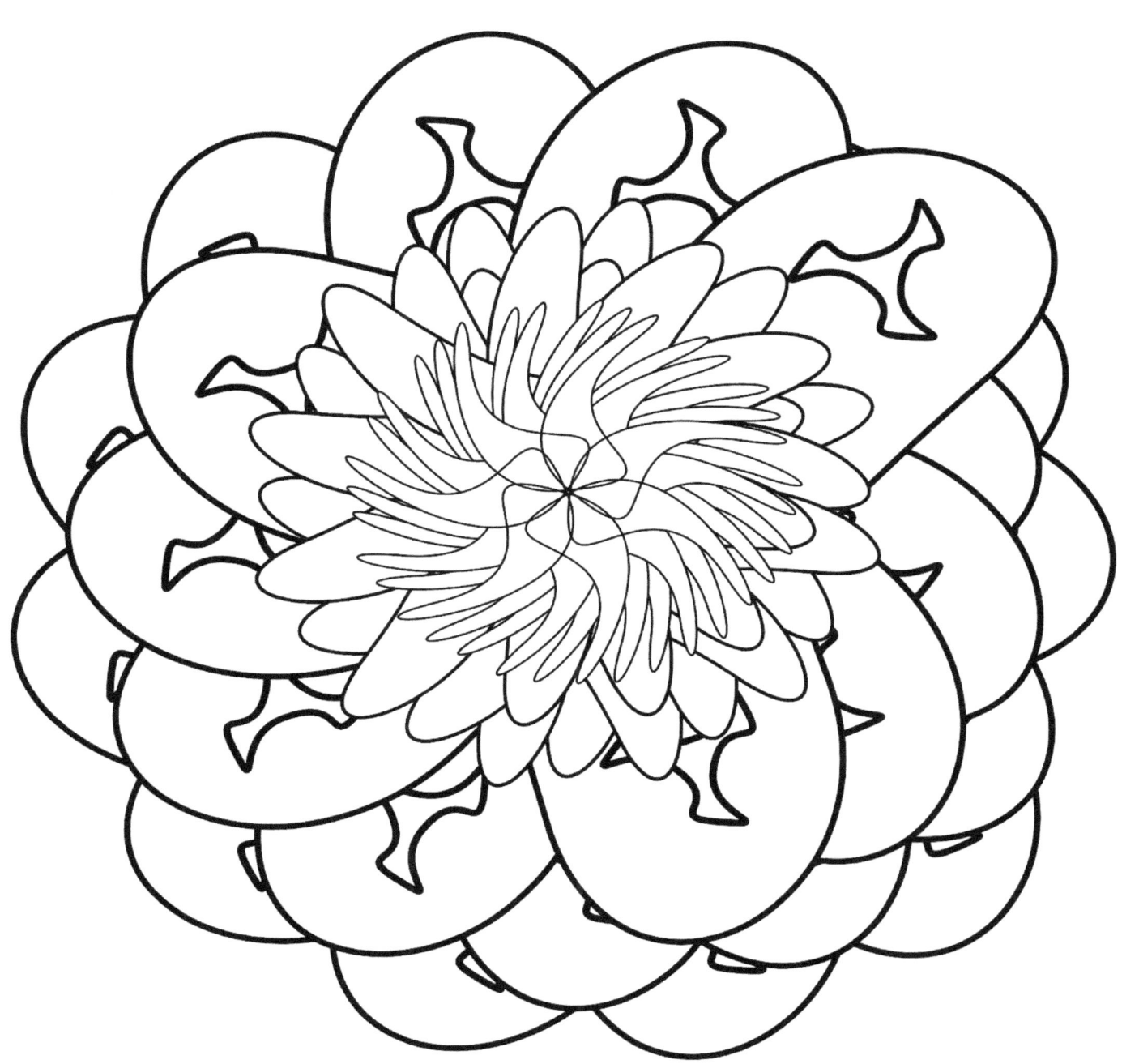

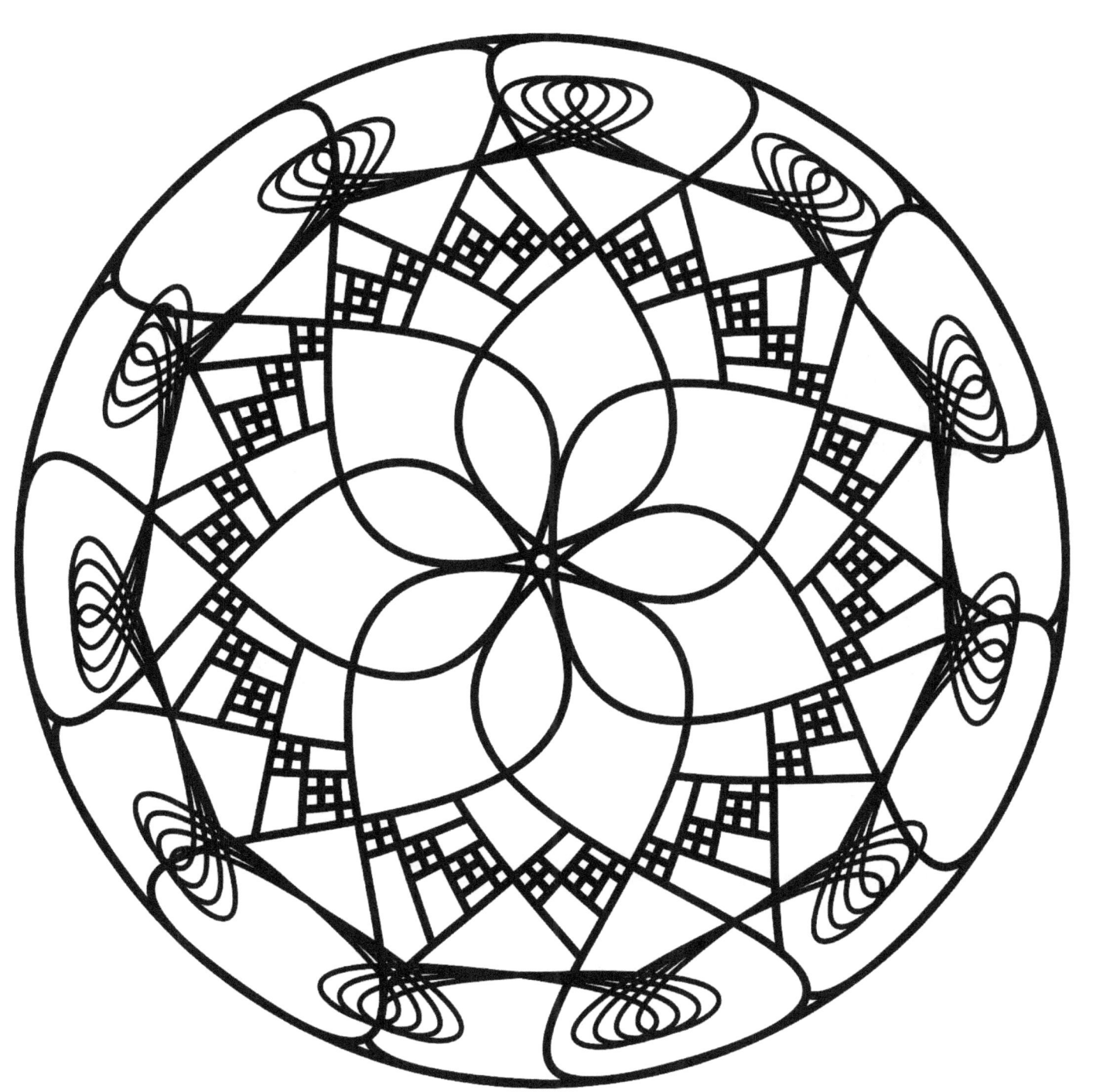

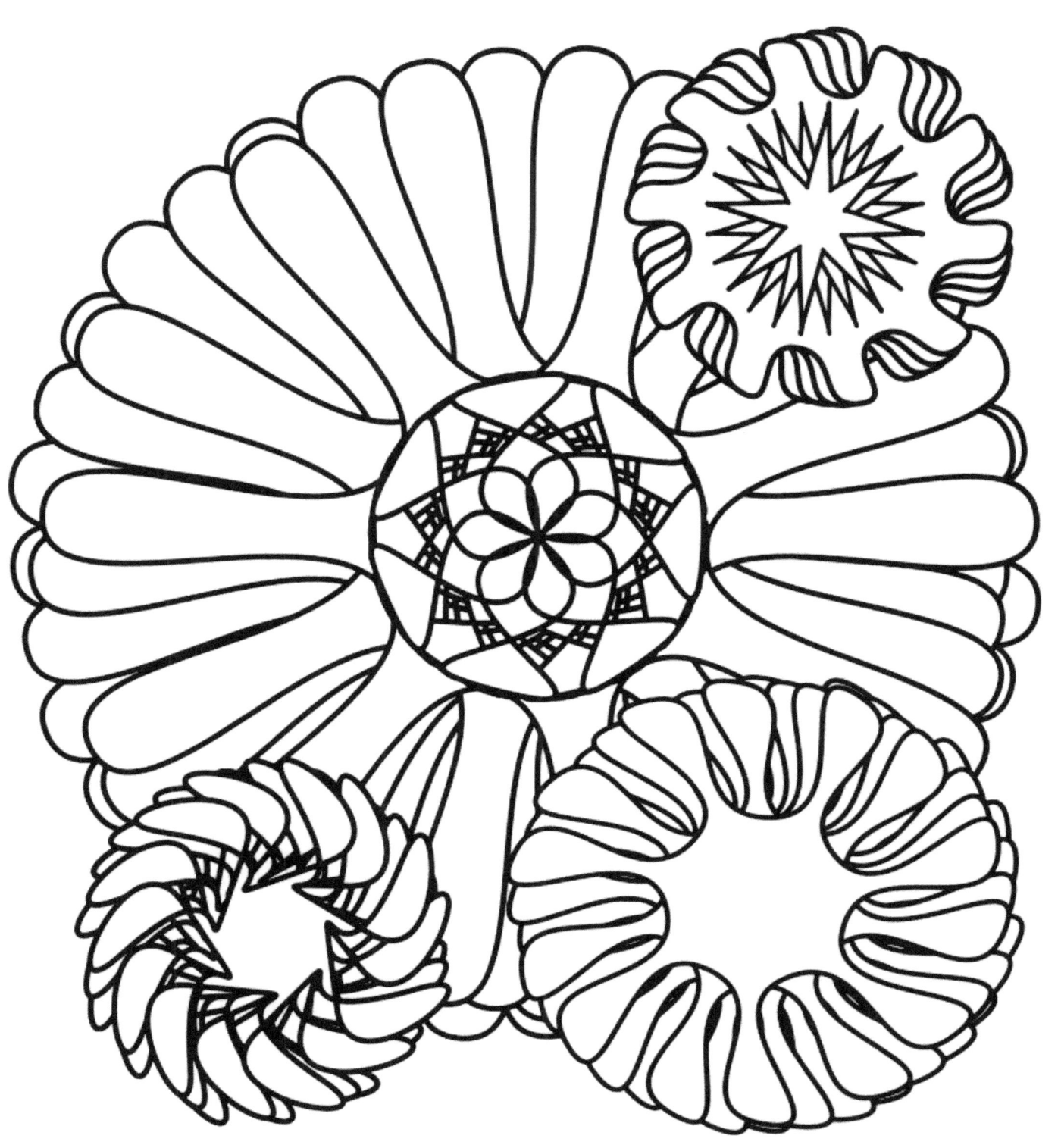

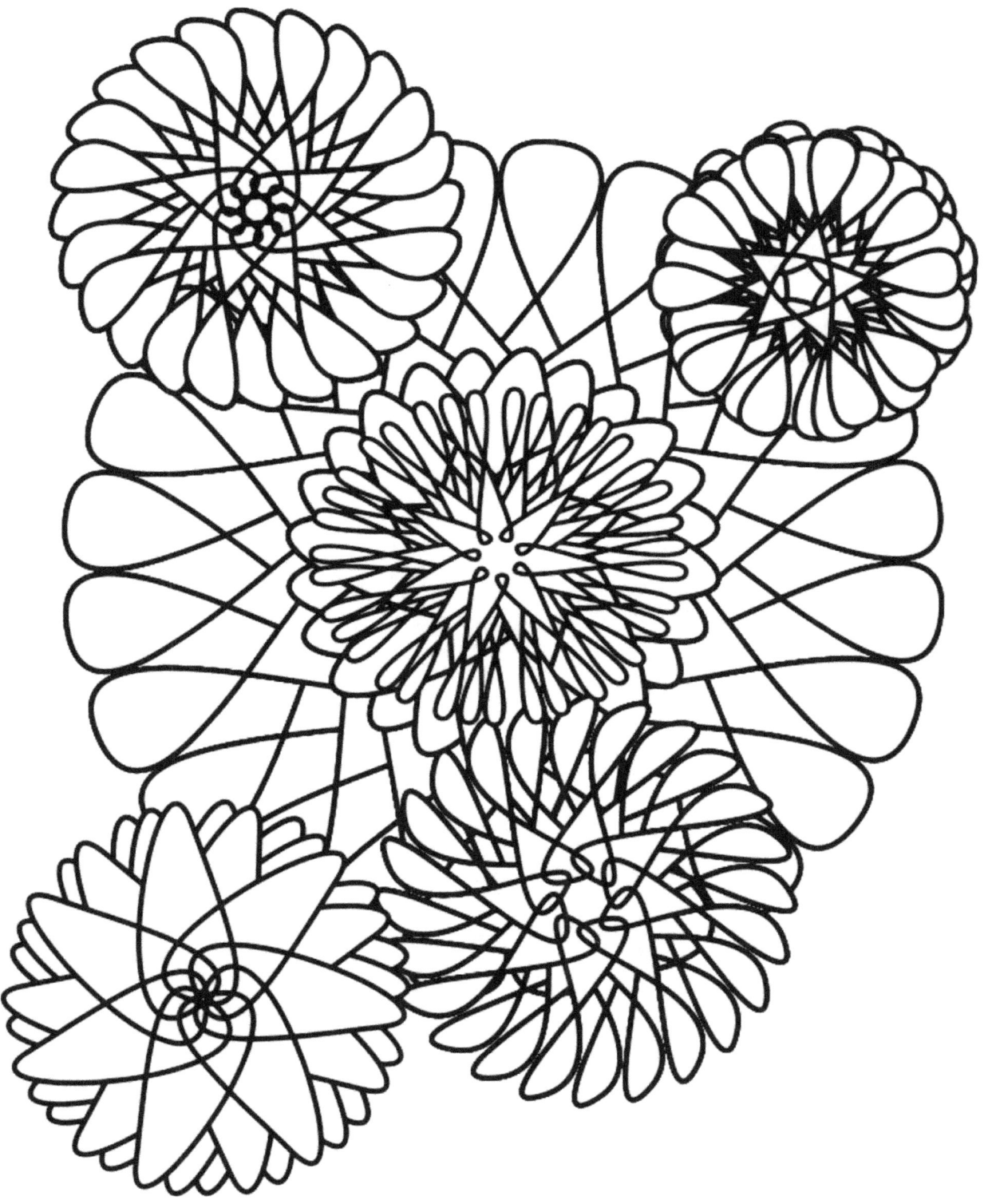

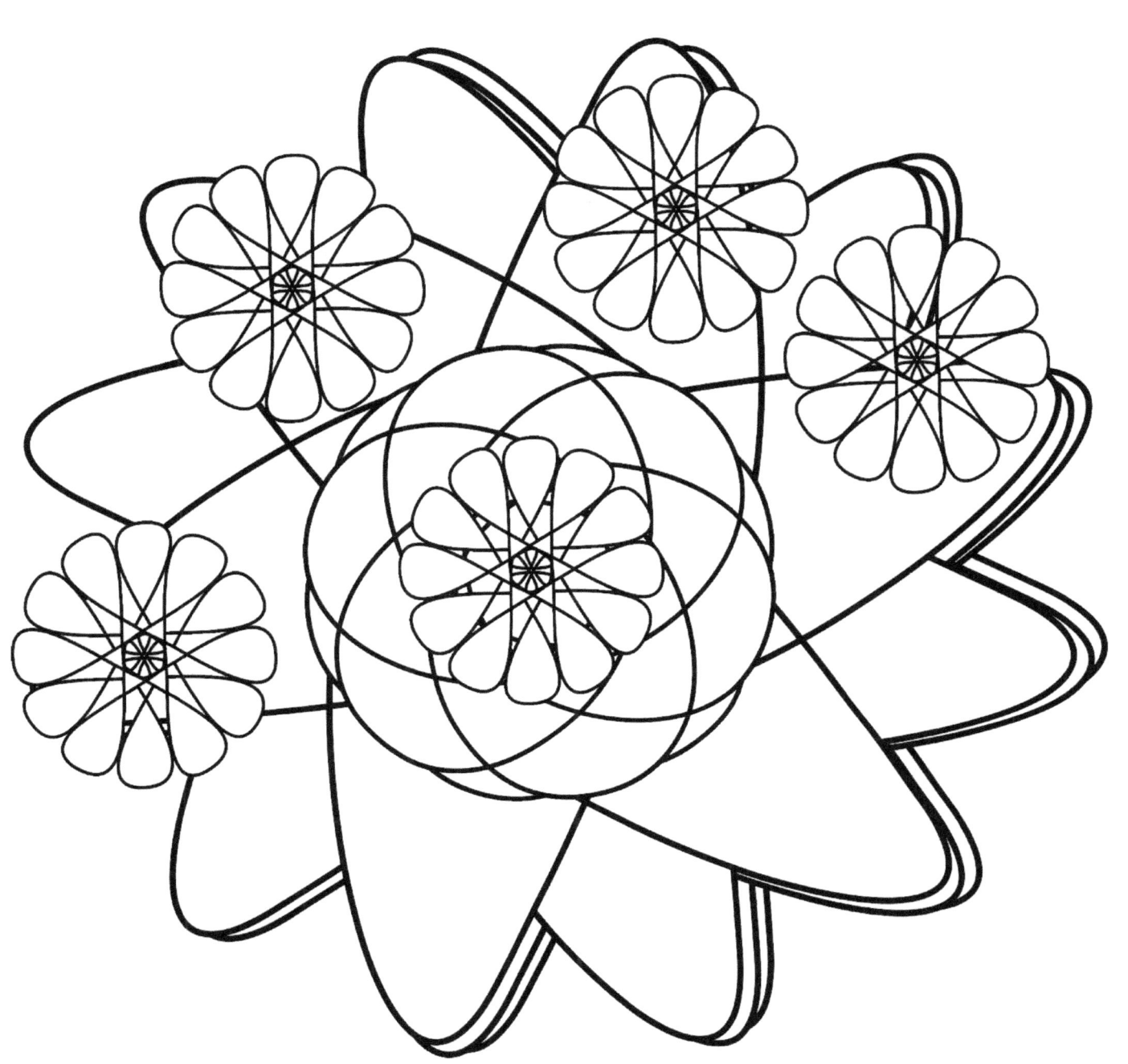

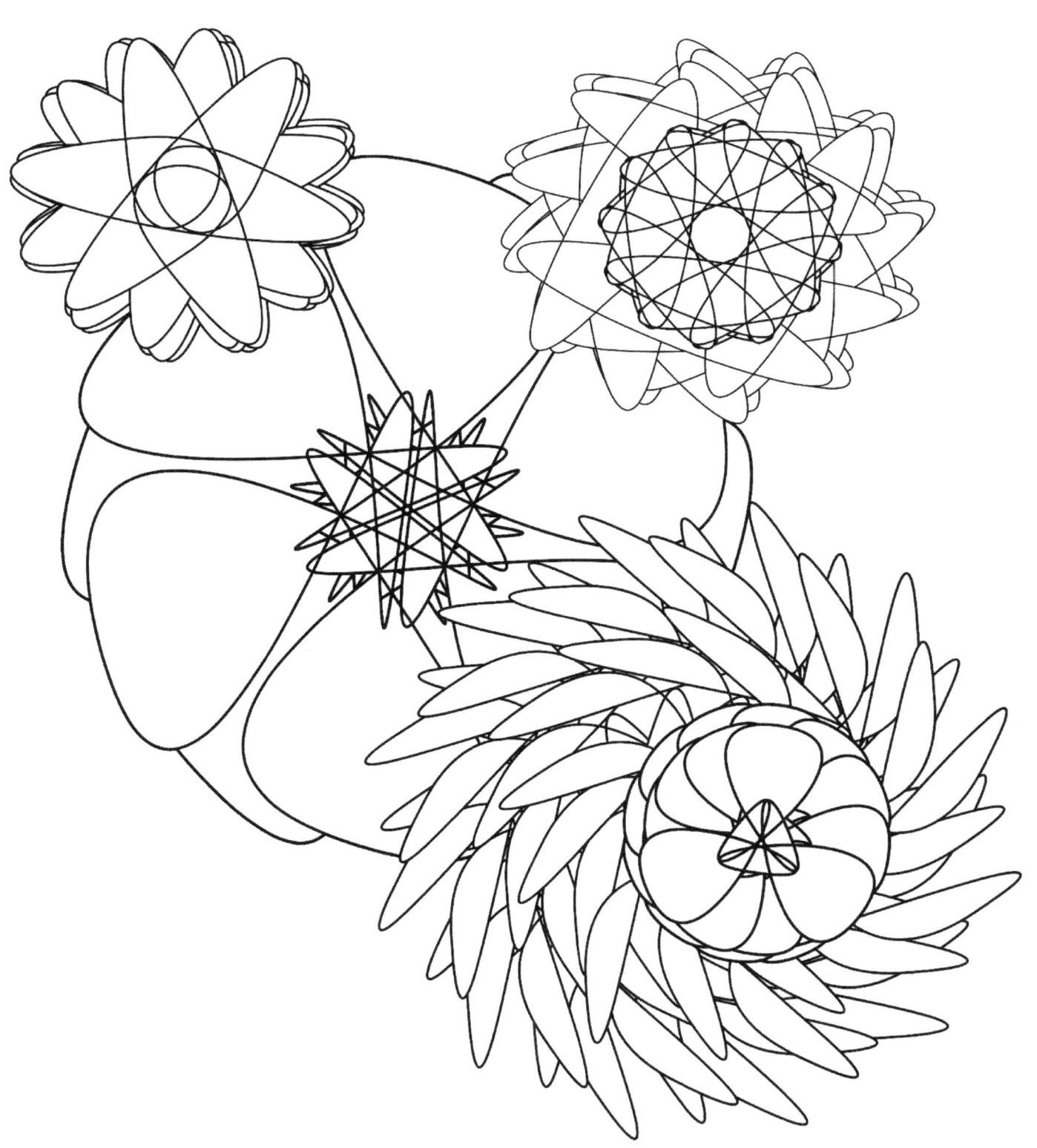

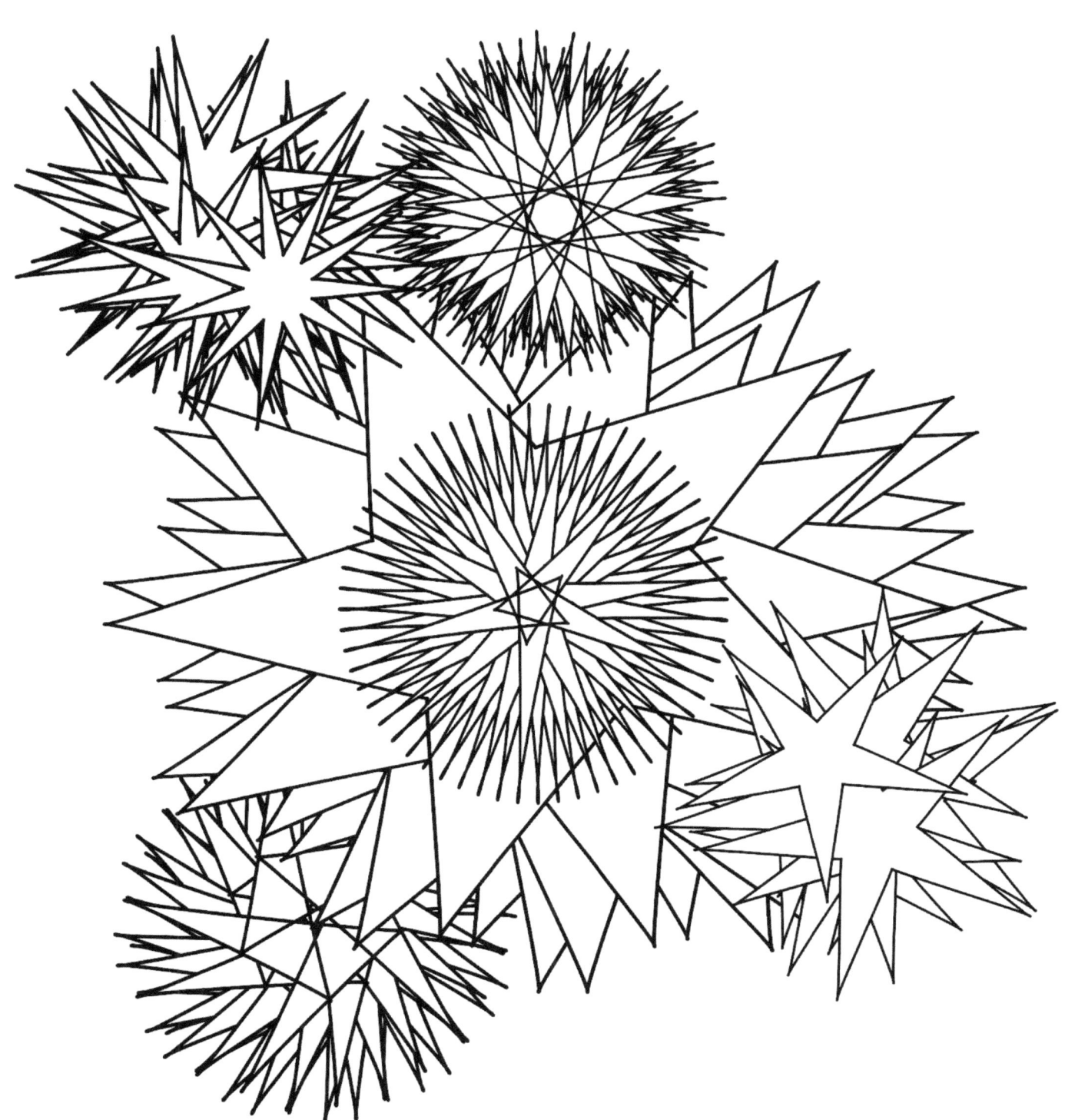

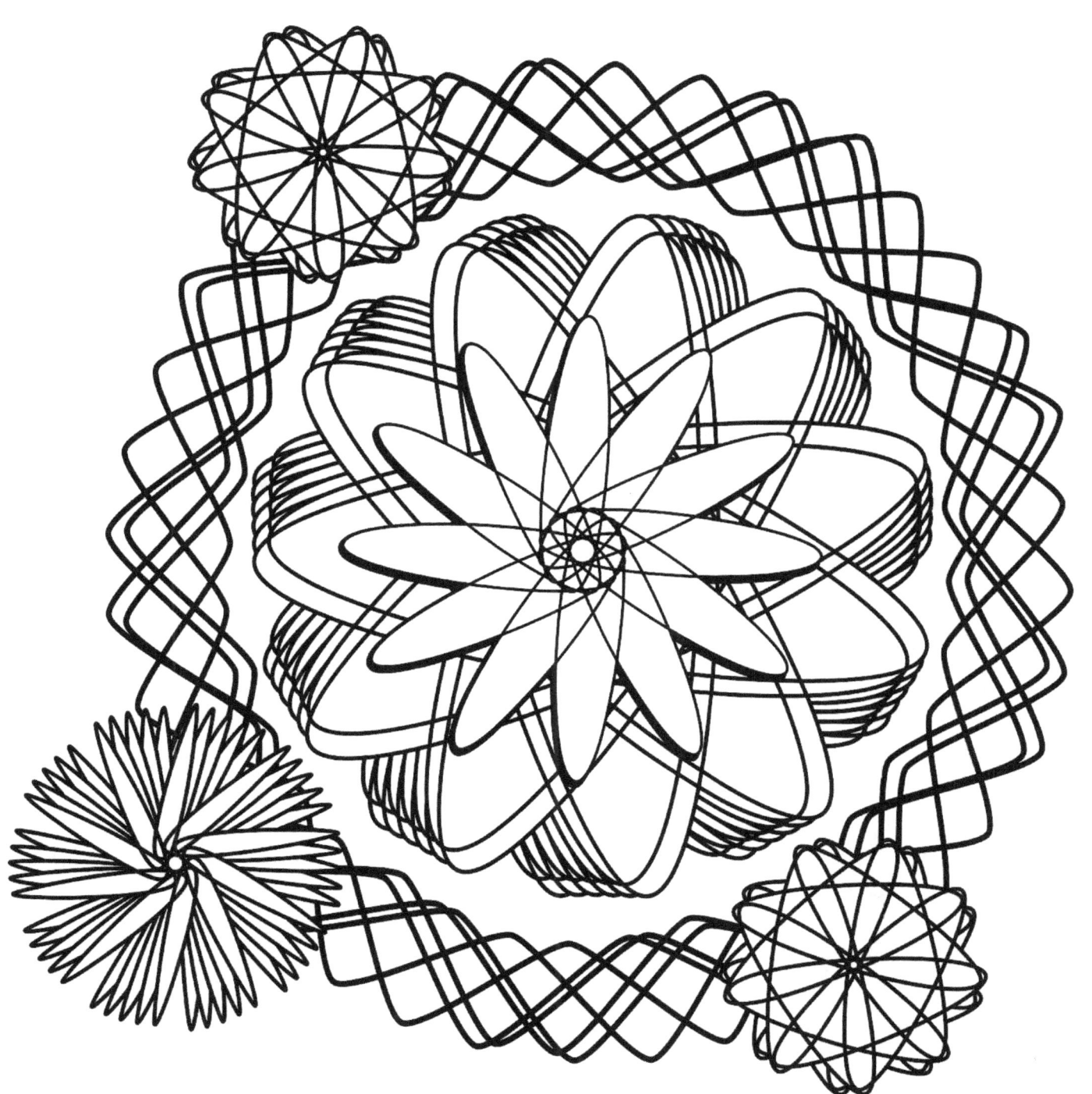

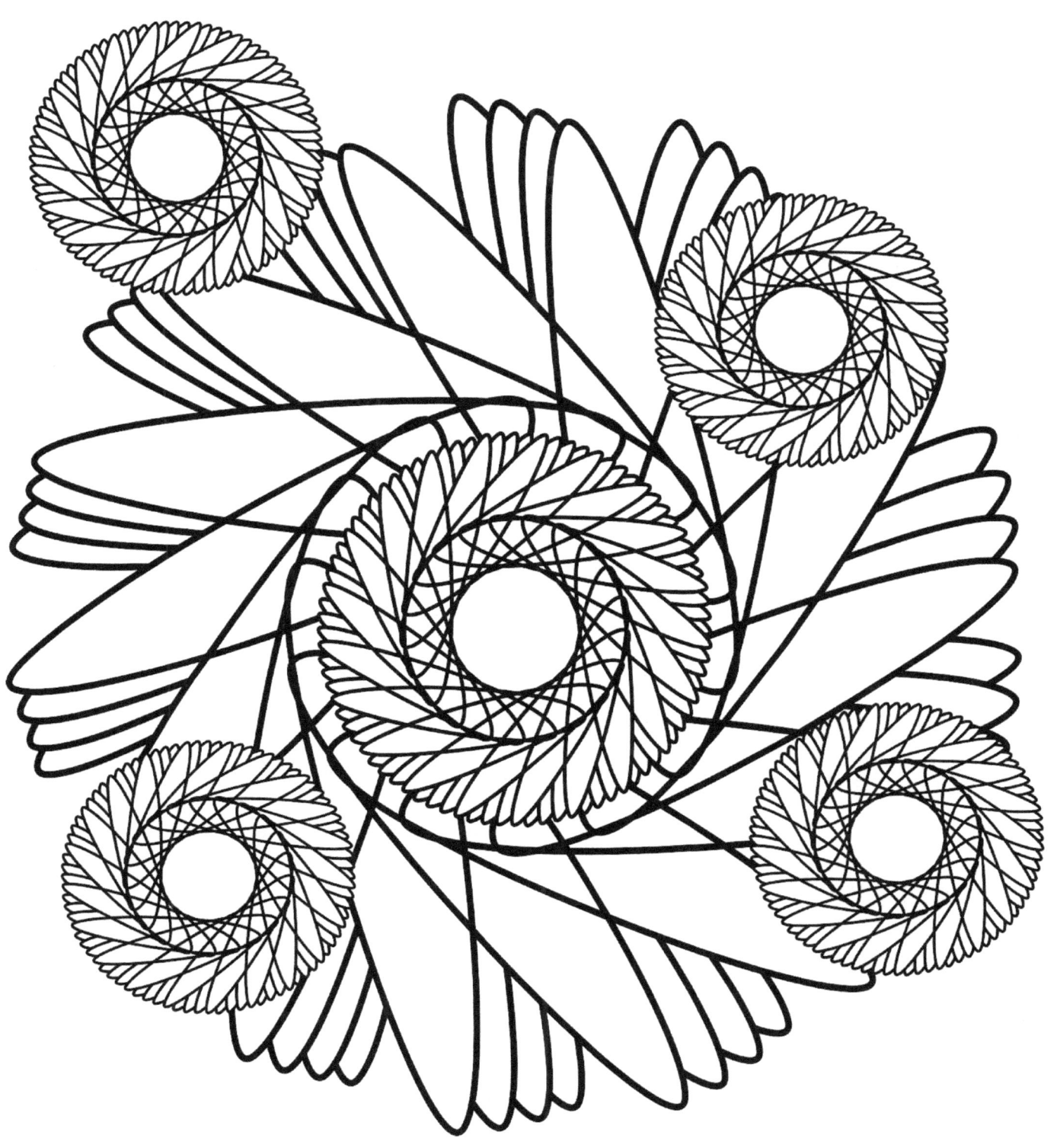

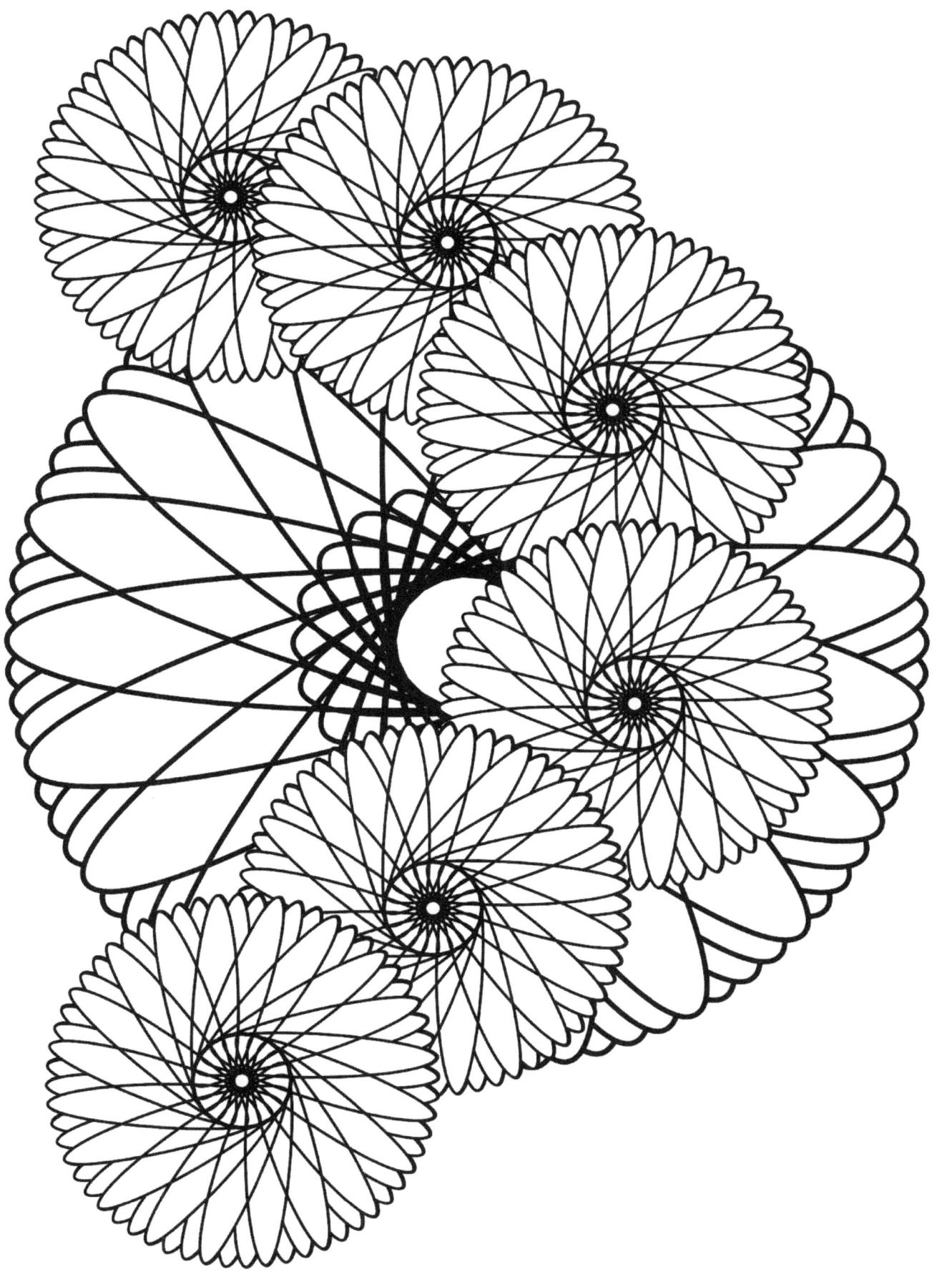

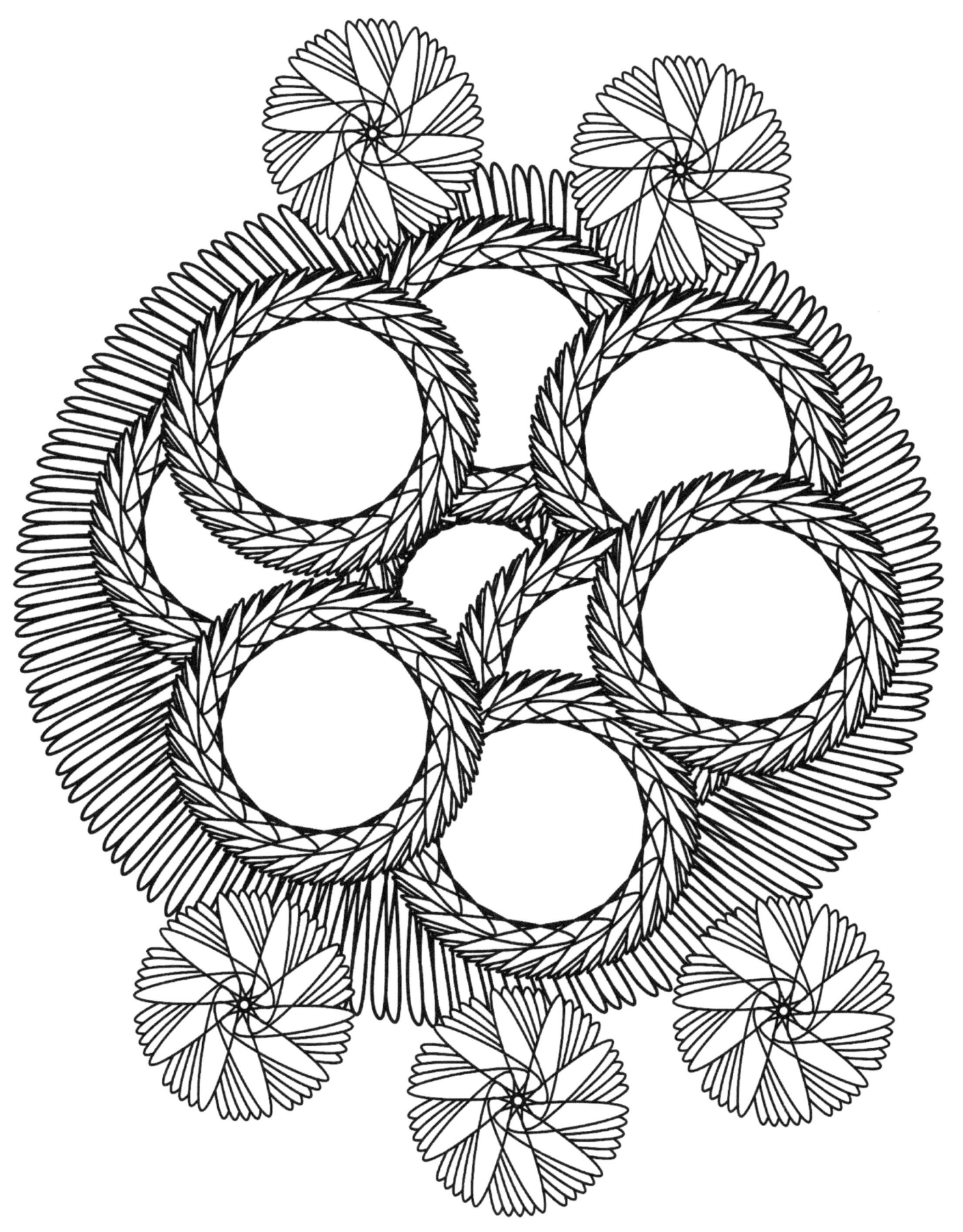

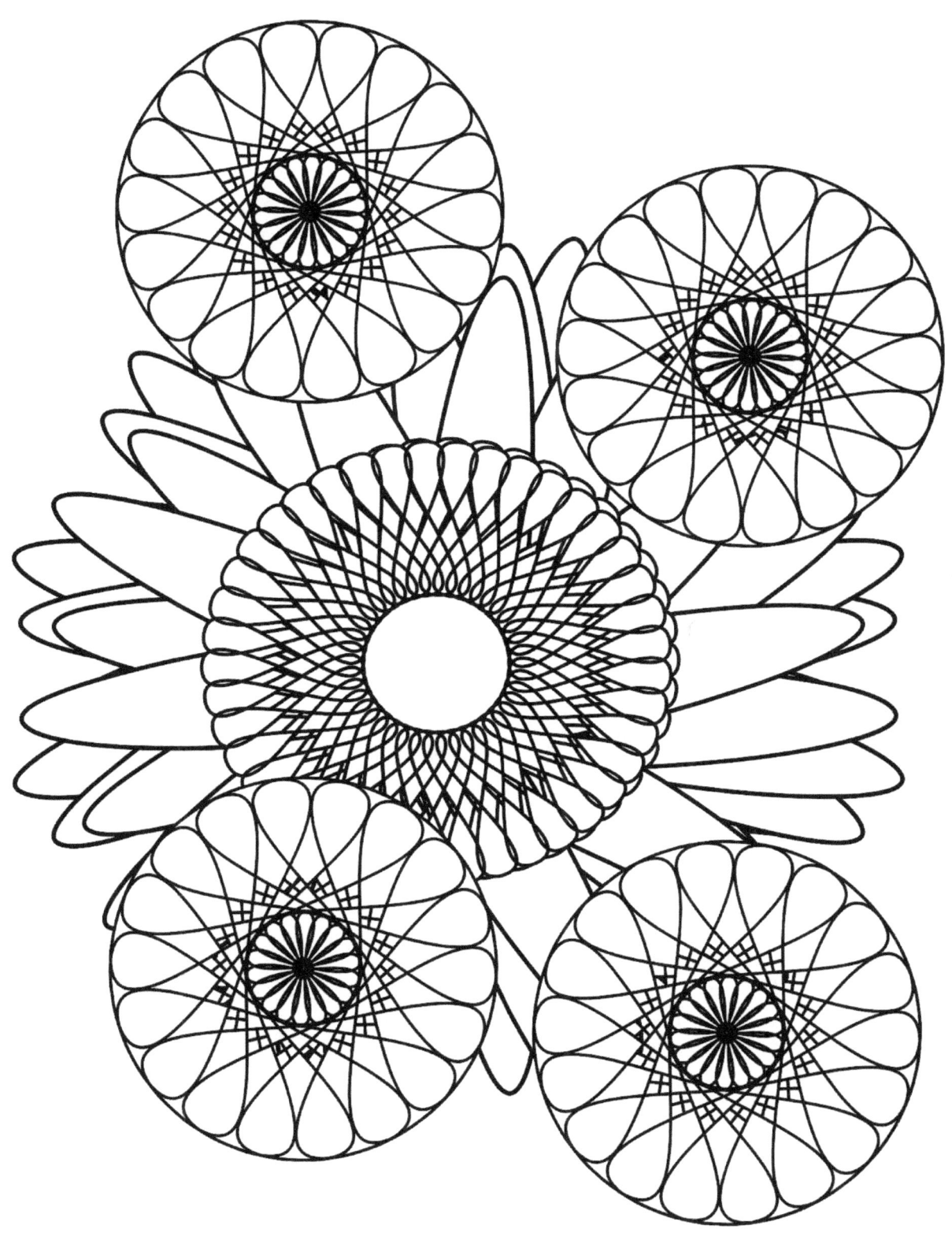

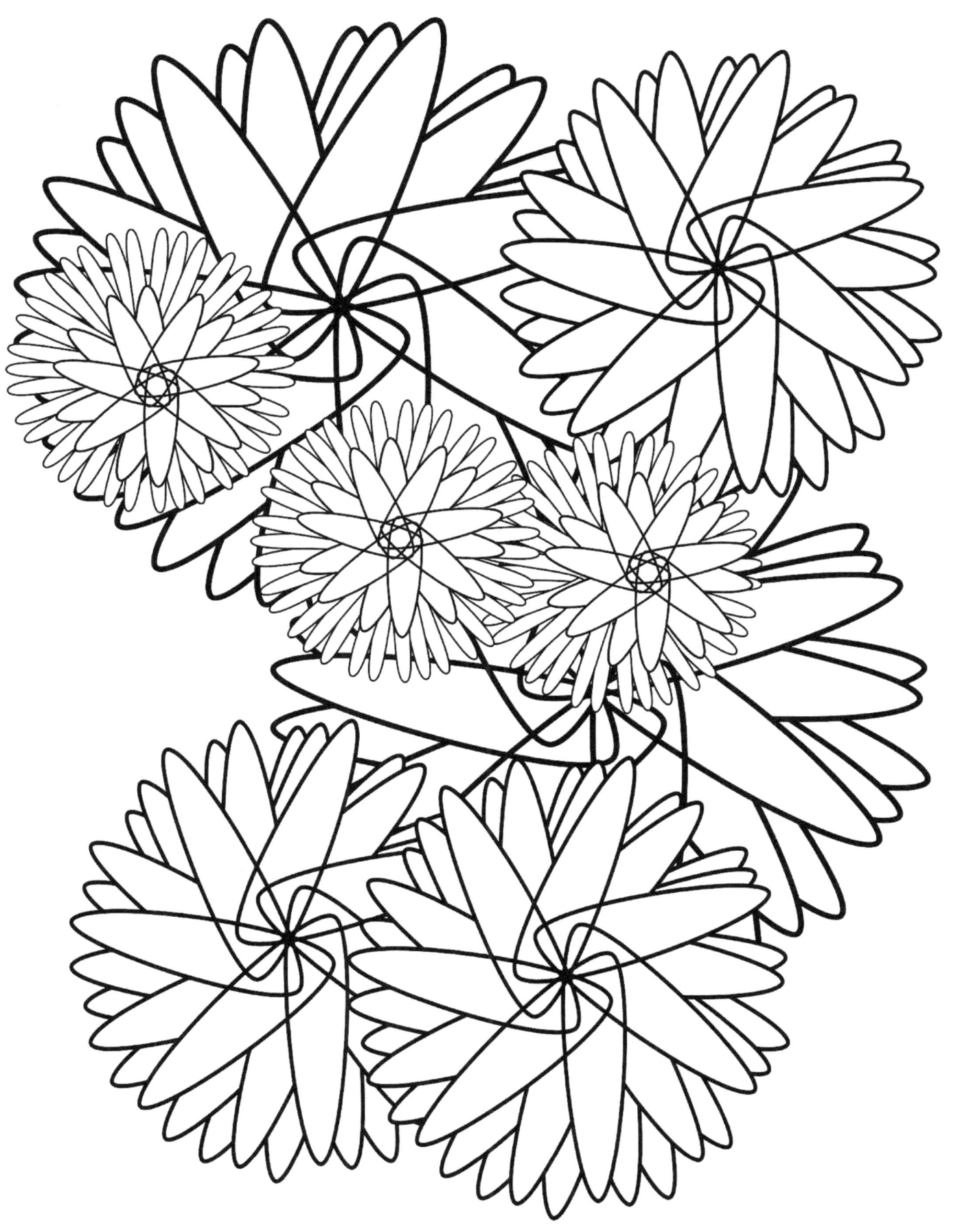

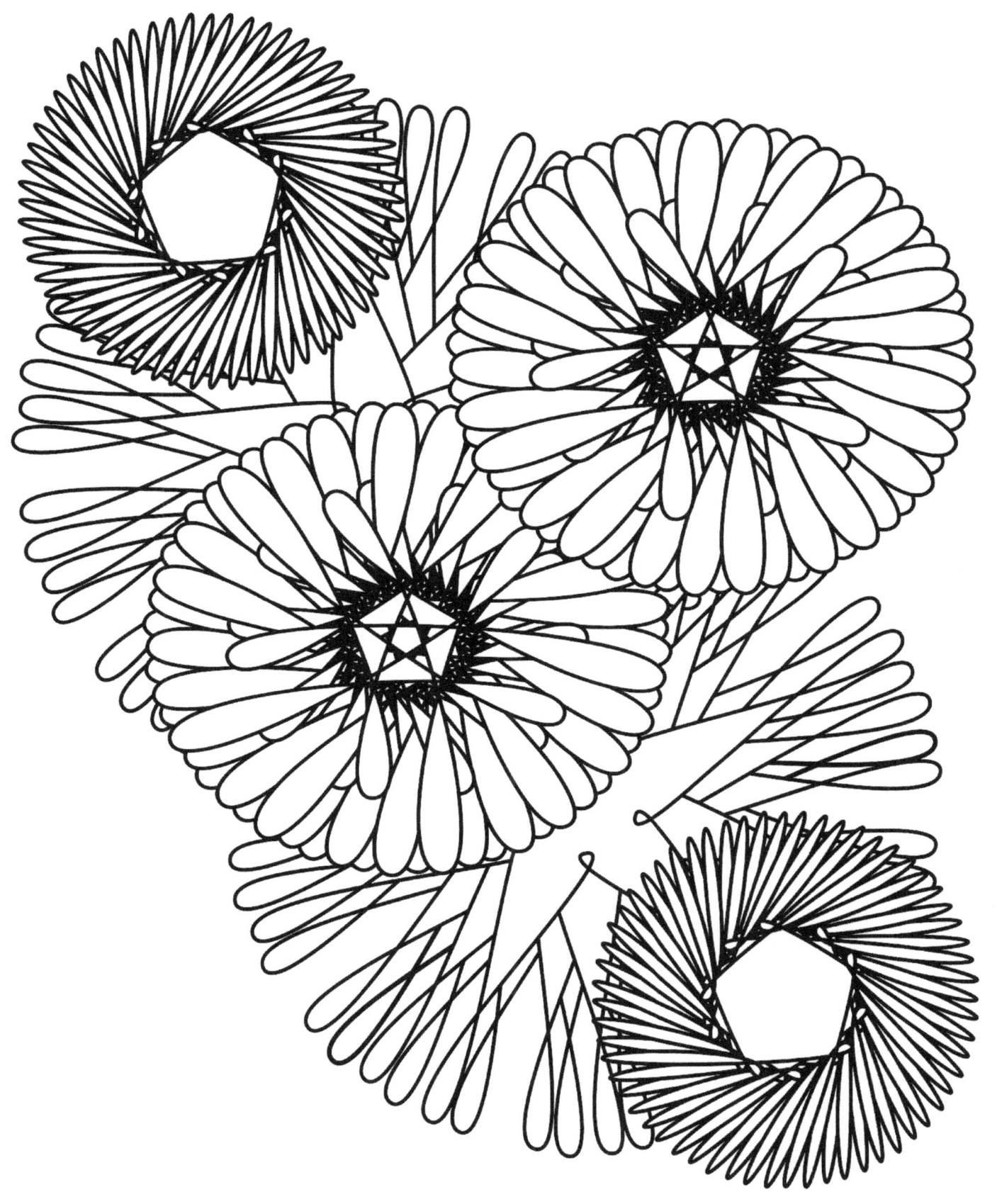